Weird Wonders of the Deep
An Imagination Library Series

Whale Sharks

by Valerie J. Weber

GARETH**STEVENS**
PUBLISHING
A WRC Media Company

Please visit our web site at: www.garethstevens.com
For a free color catalog describing Gareth Stevens Publishing's
list of high-quality books and multimedia programs,
call 1-800-542-2595 (USA) or 1-800-387-3178 (Canada).
Gareth Stevens Publishing's fax: (414) 332-3567.

Library of Congress Cataloging-in-Publication Data

Weber, Valerie.
    Whale sharks / by Valerie J. Weber.
        p. cm. — (Weird wonders of the deep: an imagination library series)
    Includes bibliographical references and index.
    ISBN 0-8368-4565-X (lib. bdg.)
    1. Whale shark—Juvenile literature. I. Title.
    QL638.95.R4W44   2005
    597.3—dc22   2004062580

First published in 2005 by
Gareth Stevens Publishing
A WRC Media Company
330 West Olive Street, Suite 100
Milwaukee, WI 53212 USA

Cover design and page layout: Scott M. Krall
Series editors: JoAnn Early Macken and Mark J. Sachner
Picture Researcher: Diane Laska-Swanke

Photo credits: Cover © Mark Strickland/SeaPics.com; pp. 5, 11, 21 © James D. Watt/SeaPics.com;
p. 7 © Franco Banfi/SeaPics.com; p. 9 © Steve Drogin/SeaPics.com; p. 13 © Chris & Monique
Fallows/SeaPics.com; p. 15 © Bob Cranston/SeaPics.com; pp. 17, 19 © Graeme Teague

Printed in the United States of America

1 2 3 4 5 6 7 8 9 09 08 07 06 05

Front cover: A gentle giant, the whale shark swims in warm
seas throughout the world. Just like every person has
different fingerprints, every whale shark has different markings.

Table of Contents

Words that appear in the glossary are printed in **boldface** type the first time they occur in the text.

The Look-Alike

What looks like a whale, swims like a whale, and feeds like a whale but isn't a whale?

Answer? A whale shark!

Because of its huge size and large mouth, a whale shark may look like a whale. It is not a **mammal** like a true whale is, however. Whale sharks gather **oxygen** from the water they swim through. Whales breathe oxygen from the air like people do.

This spotted giant swims near the surface, looking for food. Many other sharks live on or near the bottom of the ocean.

A Big Gulp

Imagine a sunny, calm day in warm seas far from shore. Big clouds of **plankton** hover at the water's surface. Suddenly, a huge mouth, 6 feet (almost 2 meters) wide, breaks above the water. As it rises higher, water streams from the creature's **gills**. The plankton disappears down the huge animal's throat.

You have just seen the largest fish in the world feeding on some of its smallest creatures. The longest whale shark measured stretched to 40 feet (12 m). Scientists think whale sharks can grow to nearly 60 feet (18 m). They can weigh twice as much as an elephant — up to 27,000 pounds (12,200 kilograms) — or more. An adult person could comfortably lie down inside a whale shark's broad mouth.

It is hard to guess the weight of these huge animals. Scientists thought one whale shark caught in 1994 weighed 79,000 pounds (36,000 kg)!

Too Big to Bother

That immense size serves several purposes.
First, few **predators** grow large enough to threaten
whale sharks. Its only enemy might be the adult
great white shark, which can grow up to 25 feet
(nearly 8 m) long.

Second, its large mouth allows it to gather a lot
of tiny plants and animals to feed on. Third, if food
is scarce, the whale shark can live off the energy
stored in its fat until it can swim to new food sources.
Scientists tracked one whale for forty months. It
covered 14,000 miles (22,500 kilometers), swimming
nearly twice the distance around the world!

Golden pilot jack fish swim inside this whale
shark's mouth. Even tiny fish like these provide
part of a meal for a monster.

Not Your Usual Shark

When you think of a shark, you probably think of a sleek, fast hunter. The whale shark is quite different than the typical shark, however. While most sharks chase after their **prey**, the whale shark can feed slowly among the plankton.

Most kinds of sharks have their mouths underneath their heads. The whale shark's broad mouth stretches across the front of its head.

Although a powerful swimmer, cruising at 3 to 5 miles (5 to 8 km) per hour, the whale shark is no match for other sharks. For example, the mako shark can swim 20 miles (32 m) per hour. In short bursts, the mako can go twice or three times that fast.

Open wide! You could drive a sports car through a whale shark's mouth.

A Toothy Grin

Razor-sharp teeth fill the mouths of most sharks, but not the whale shark. Its fifteen thousand teeth are tiny, about 1/8 of an inch long (.3 centimeter). Three hundred rows of teeth line each jaw just inside the whale shark's lips.

While its teeth are not suited to grasping prey, they do help trap food in the whale shark's mouth as water rushes out. Nothing larger than .08 to .12 inches (2 to 3 millimeters) escapes. Whale sharks dine on fish **larvae**, squid, sardines, and plankton. They also eat krill, which are tiny animals that look like shrimp.

This great white shark's sharp teeth chomp into a dead whale. Most sharks have pointy teeth like these and eat larger prey than the whale shark does.

A Giant Vacuum Cleaner

As the giant shark swims slowly through the water, it turns its head back and forth. It opens and closes its wide mouth, sucking in thousands of gallons of seawater every day.

Alongside of its mouth run five huge gill slits. They look like thick, polka-dot ribbons attached to the upper and lower sides of its body. (Only the basking shark sports larger gills.) The gills filter oxygen from the water and help strain food from it as well.

Attached to these gills inside the whale shark's mouth are rakers. Rakers are made from hard tissue called **cartilage**. The rakers also strain food from the water and sweep it down to the shark's narrow throat.

Above the whale shark's wide mouth lie its nostrils. The whale shark moves its head back and forth to help smell its prey.

A Mystery Solved

For many years, scientists argued over how baby whale sharks were born. Some thought that a whale shark laid eggs onto the ocean floor. Inside, the eggs developed fully formed babies. Others believed that the female whale shark kept her eggs inside her until the baby sharks were strong enough to break out of the eggs themselves. The mother would then push the live sharks from her body.

In 1995, a female whale shark was killed with nearly three hundred **embryos** inside her. The embryos were at different stages of growing into baby sharks. They ranged in size from 16 to 24 inches (42 to 63 cm) long. Scientists decided from this discovery that whale sharks did indeed keep their eggs inside until the babies hatched out.

Remoras keep this whale shark company. These fish clean tiny animals and plants from the shark's hide.

Born to Swim

While the mother whale shark may have hundreds of eggs, not all of those eggs grow into whale sharks. Often, the strongest baby sharks break out of their eggs first. They start to eat the eggs and weaker baby sharks nearby — all while in their mother's body.

Baby whale sharks are called pups. They can live on their own from the minute they are born. They have to. Like other sharks, mother whale sharks sometimes eat their own babies.

Divers swim with a young whale shark. This youngster may live to be one hundred years old. Whale sharks can live longer than most other animals on earth.

Gentle Giants

Whale sharks are not a danger to humans. The most damage that can be done comes when a fishing or diving boat meets a whale shark head. While the boat may bob, the fish comes off the worst. Some whale sharks carry scars from this kind of meeting.

Divers can grab onto whale sharks and go for a ride through the **tropical** seas. If the shark wants them off, it simply heads down to deeper water where people can't stand the pressure.

A diver hitches a ride on a whale shark. Remoras swim beneath it, hoping for scraps from its next meal.

More to Read and View

Books (Nonfiction)   *Sharks.* Amanda Harman and Casey Horton
                                (Marshall Cavendish Inc.)
                             The Whale Shark. Creatures of the Sea (series). Kris Hirschmann
                                (Kidhaven Press)
                             The Whale Shark. The Underwater World of Sharks (series).
                                Brad Burnham (The Rosen Publishing Group)
                             Whale Sharks. Anne Welsbacher (Capstone Press)
                             Whale Sharks. Sharks (series). John F. Prevost
                                (Abdo Publishing Company)

Videos (Nonfiction)   *Whale Shark Hunters.* (Pro-Active Entertain)

Places to Write and Visit

Here are three places to contact for more information:

Mystic Aquarium and   **Monterey Bay Aquarium**   **John G. Shedd Aquarium**
Institute for Exploration   886 Cannery Row   1200 South Lake Shore Drive
55 Coogan Boulevard   Monterey, CA 93940   Chicago, IL 60605
Mystic, CT 06355-1997

Web Sites

Web sites change frequently, but we believe the following web sites are going to last. You can also use good search engines, such as **Yahooligans!** [www.yahooligans.com] or **Google** [www.google.com], to find more information about whale sharks. Here are some keywords to help you: *sharks, largest fish, rakers,* and *whale shark pups.*

animaldiversity.ummz.umich.edu/site/ accounts/information/Rhincodon_typus. html
The University of Michigan's Animal Diversity web site gives precise scientific information on the whale shark.

library.thinkquest.org/CR0215242/ sharks.htm
Children developed this web site on sharks. Though it does not refer specifically to whale sharks, it contains a lot of information on sharks in general.

www.EnchantedLearning.com/subjects/ sharks
Check out this web site for a fact sheet on whale sharks. You can also learn more general information about sharks here.

www.sheddaquarium.org/sea/fact_sheets_ print.cfm?id=64
The Shedd Aquarium in Chicago provides a fact sheet with interesting information on whale sharks.

www.whaletimes.org/whshark.htm
Click on this web site for facts about whale sharks. You can also look up other sea creatures here.

www.worldwildlife.org/expeditions/reef/ index.html
This World Wildlife Organization's web site can take you on an expedition to the Mesoamerican Reef, the largest Atlantic Ocean coral system and the home of whale sharks and their neighbors.

Glossary

You can find these words on the pages listed. Reading a word in a sentence helps you understand it even better.

cartilage (KAHR-til-ihj) — a tough, stretchy material found in many animals' bodies. Your ears have cartilage beneath the skin. 14

embryos (EM-bree-oes) — animals that are just starting to live and grow, before their birth 16

gills (GILS) — the part of a fish used for breathing. Gills take in oxygen from the water. 6, 14

larvae (LAHR-vae) — animals in a newly hatched, early stage before they change into adults. 12

mammal (MAM-uhl) — a kind of animal that is warm-blooded and has a backbone. A female mammal feeds her young with milk that her body produces. 4

oxygen (AHK-suh-jen) — a colorless gas that has no smell that people and animals need to live 4, 14

plankton (PLANK-tuhn) — tiny plants and animals that float in fresh- or saltwater, especially on the surface. Plankton is a basic food in the ocean that many animals depend on to live. 6, 10, 12

predators (PRED-uh-turz) — animals that hunt other animals for food 8

prey (PRAY) — animal that are hunted by other animals for food 10, 12

tropical (TROP-ih-cull) being in part of the world where the temperature is always warm and plants usually grow year-round 20

Index